Seahorse Fry

by Ruth Owen

Consultant:
David Wedge
Senior Aquarist
Wet Lab & Edge of the Sea Exhibit
New England Aquarium
Boston, Massachusetts

BEARPORT
PUBLISHING

New York, New York

Credits

Cover and Title Page, © Felicia McCaulley and totophotos/Shutterstock; 4–5, © Doug Perrine/seapics.com; 6, © Cosmographics; 7, © Michael Patrick O'Neill/Photoshot; 9L, © David Kearnes/seapics.com; 9R, © Gregory G. Dimijian/Photoshot; 11, © George Grall/National Geographic/Getty Images; 13, © Doug Perrine/Nature Picture Library; 14–15, © Doug Perrine/Nature Picture Library; 16, © Felicia McCaulley; 17, © Studio 37/ Shutterstock; 19, © Marc Bernardi/seapics.com; 21, © Steven Kovacs/seapics.com; 22T, © Marc Bernardi/seapics.com; 22C, © Doug Perrine/Nature Picture Library; 22B, © Jamie Craggs/Papilio/Alamy; 23T, © George Grall/National Geographic/Getty Images; 23C, © Doug Perrine/Nature Picture Library; 23B, © Suphatthra China/Shutterstock.

Publisher: Kenn Goin
Senior Editor: Lisa Wiseman
Creative Director: Spencer Brinker
Design: Emma Randall
Editor: Mark J Sachner
Photo Researcher: Ruby Tuesday Books Ltd

Library of Congress Cataloging-in-Publication Data

Owen, Ruth, 1967–
  Seahorse fry / by Ruth Owen.
      p. cm.
  Audience: 6–9.
  Includes bibliographical references and index.
  ISBN 978-1-61772-604-0 (library binding) — ISBN 1-61772-604-4 (library binding)
 1. Sea horses—Juvenile literature. 2. Sea horses—Infancy—Juvenile literature. I.
Title.
  QL638.S9O94 2013
  597′.6798—dc23

                                        2012021238

For more information, write to Bearport Publishing Company, Inc., 45 West 21st Street, Suite 3B, New York, New York 10010. Printed in the United States of America.

10 9 8 7 6 5 4 3 2 1

Contents

Meet some seahorse fry

Two tiny creatures are swimming together.

They are using their tails to hold onto each other.

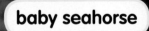
baby seahorse

The little animals are seahorse babies, or **fry**.

They have just been born and are only a few seconds old!

tails

Where do seahorses live?

Seahorses live in the ocean among grasses and seaweed.

There are many different types of seahorses.

Lined seahorses live in the places shown on the map.

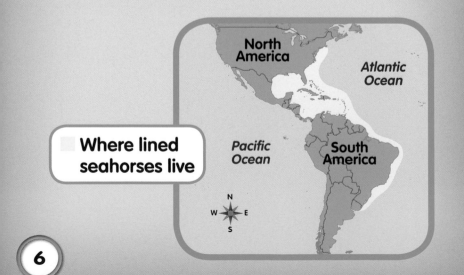

Where lined seahorses live

North America

Atlantic Ocean

Pacific Ocean

South America

N W E S

Seahorses may look a little like tiny horses, but they are actually fish.

adult lined seahorse

seaweed

All about lined seahorses

Adult lined seahorses can be brown, gray, yellow, orange, or red.

They get their name because they sometimes have stripes, or lines, on their skin.

Unlike other fish, a seahorse doesn't have a **skeleton** made up of bones.

It has a skeleton of hard, bony sections that are joined together, like **armor**.

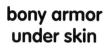

bony armor
under skin

lines

Adult lined
seahorse size

pencil

A seahorse pair

A male and a female seahorse live together for their whole lives.

Every morning, they curl their tails together and dance around in the water.

When the seahorses are ready to **mate**, they put their bodies together.

Then the female sprays hundreds of eggs into a **pouch** on the male's body.

dancing male
and female
seahorses

Here come the babies!

About 15 days after the male and female mate, the seahorse fry **hatch** inside their father's pouch.

They live in the pouch for about five days.

When they are strong enough to swim, the father bends his body backward and forward.

As he pushes his body forward, tiny seahorse babies pop out of his pouch!

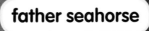

father seahorse

pouch

seahorse fry

Tiny seahorses

The father and mother seahorses do not take care of their babies.

As soon as the tiny fry leave their father's body, they swim off.

The babies look a lot like their parents, but they are much smaller.

Each tiny seahorse is less than half an inch (1.3 cm) long.

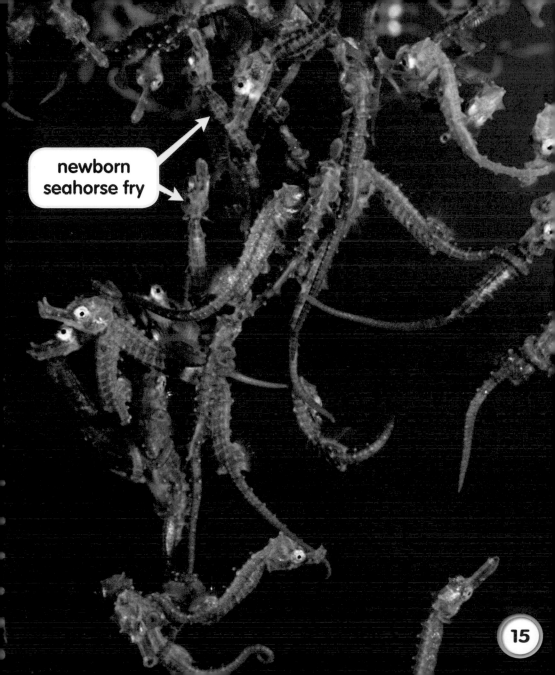

newborn seahorse fry

Life in the ocean

Like adult seahorses, the fry spend their days swimming in the ocean.

They use their fins to help them move through the water.

fin

newborn seahorse fry

When they rest, seahorses often use their tails to hold onto seaweed or grasses.

This stops them from being washed away from their home area by waves.

tail

Seahorse food

Seahorse adults and fry eat tiny ocean animals such as shrimp.

To get food, a seahorse waits for its meal to swim by.

Then it sucks in the animal, using its snout like a vacuum cleaner!

An adult seahorse eats about 50 shrimp in a day.

A growing baby seahorse eats thousands of shrimp in a day.

snout

Growing up

The seahorse fry grow bigger and bigger.

It takes about eight months for them to grow into adults.

Once they are grown up, they find partners and become part of a seahorse pair.

Then, the young seahorses are ready to have fry of their own!

a seahorse pair

Glossary

armor (AR-mur)
a hard covering that
protects a body

fry (FRYE)
baby fish

hatch (HACH)
to break out
of an egg

mate (MAYT)
to come together
to have young

pouch (POUCH)
part of a male seahorse's
body where his fry hatch
from their eggs

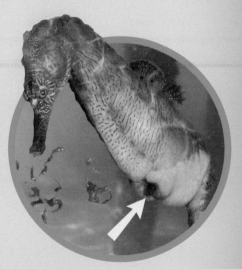

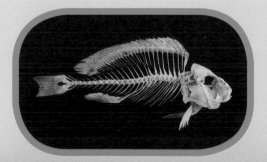

skeleton (SKEL-uh-tuhn)
the bones of an animal
that protect and support
its body

Index

Read more

James, Sylvia M. *Seahorses.* New York: Mondo (2002).

Kalman, Bobbie. *The Life Cycle of a Seahorse (The Life Cycle Series).* New York: Crabtree (2004).

Rhodes, Mary Jo, and David Hall. *Seahorses and Sea Dragons (Undersea Encounters).* New York: Scholastic (2005).

Learn more online

To learn more about seahorses, visit **www.bearportpublishing.com/WaterBabies**

About the author

Ruth Owen has been writing children's books for more than ten years. She particularly enjoys working on books about animals and the natural world. Ruth lives in Cornwall, England, just minutes from the ocean. She loves gardening and caring for her family of llamas.